Amy,

Possibly a little before your time but provides historical context! Includes, of course, the Isle of Wight (Mark 2)! Thank you for all your support & thoughtfulness.

Arthur

August 2018

Festival Annual 2009

Editors: Josh Jones and Frank Lampen
Art direction & design: Plan-B Studio (Steve Price and Nicolò Dante) | plan-bstudio.com
Festival Annual logo designed by: Brand 42 | brand42.co.uk

Cover photographs: Dan Wilton | danwilton.co.uk

ISBN: 978-0-9563022-0-5
A CIP Catalogue record for this book is available from the British Library.

Conceived, created and published by
Independents United Ltd
Tel: +44 (0)20 7748 5208
iu-hq.com
Registered Office: 27 Newman Street, London, W1T 1AR, United Kingdom

Printed and bound in Somerset by Butler Tanner and Dennis Ltd on FSC certified papers.

Festival ANNUAL 09

Independents United

THIS BOOK WAS CREATED BY:

[Maggot] / Louise Lindsay Williams, !SMEG / Lauren Smee, !![PWA]POPPY / Natalee Gray, [[NINJA!]]INDIA JANE / india warren-green, Alana Deadly, Marío untouched,!FLOWER! / Emilyjane Griffin, 4man, 4teenth, ABCAT / abzrule, abebe / Nicole Sunle, Abi / Abigail Leemin, Abi Newel, Ad / adrocks1975, adam / moby_dick1, Adam Collins, Adam Russell, Aaron Corr, Aimz / Amy Lee, Airbourne UK Fansite, Aisling Broderick, alan, Alan J Whelan, Allan Williamson, Alex / al_simmo, Alex Grimsley, Ally / Alison Malcolm, Ally / ladysilverwillow, ALTO ELITE, Am / _amandamassacre, amberly / ambercox85, Andre van Rensburg, Andrew Yacomen, ANGELFIRE PHOTOGRAPHY, angie Thomson, anish / akkoshal, Anna Rickman, Annabel Rawson, Anthony / zgw08, Antigoni Panta-Charva, Arlene Niamh Dignam, ASh GHoulmore, Automorph, Ayeeesha / Ayesha Linton Whittle, B to the ORIS / laurenrebeccabyrne, Benny Beatz, Becca Kins, Becky / Rebekah Cooke, Benjiman Gilbert, BenjyMajor, Bens, BerzerkerBlonde!, Big Cheeks, big dave / distorteddavie, Biggest Midget In The Game, Black / o_0o_0o_0o_0o_0o_0o_0o_0o, Blink~CoMa white, blondeambitiondjs, b-o-l-a-n-d-l-a-w-d / Steven Boland, Bo / xgemxgemzx, Bonnie / bonniedyball, Boyarde aka MISS QUEEN B!, BRADT, / Brad Tarbuck, Brandon / dannybrandon, Brian Bonnar, Bridie Snowdon, BROKEN FUNK, Brucky D / Bruce Van Kingsley, Butt Fairy, calv / Jordan Calvert, Caroline Dixon, Carissa Henderson, CAT / x_blindedinchains_x, Cat Clems, Catherine Welsh, Celine Haddad, Cervantes, Cessi / cessiwan, chai wallahs, Charlotte / Charlotte Perry, charlotte Holyhead, charlotte Kempster, c h a r l y / charlypopels, Chay West, .cheap thrills / Tess Harrison, Chelly Smelly, chelsie byrne, Chen!. / Chen Lockett, chirsty aggas, chocolategirl64, Chris [contrast.tv], chris haywood, Chris Leck, ChRiS / Chris Williams, Chrissy Joseph, Christian Chaos / chriswheble, Christian Pollitt, Ciara Dignam, cinderella cinderella / olivia dunn Claire Scott, Claudia James, Clayton Wright, Clover / Chloe Pattie, Connie / Constance Curtis, Control / the_just3, The Correspondents, Coxi;; BLAD / Porsche-Louise, crack / craig curtis, Craig Allen, Craig Sowerby, Curlina, Dan / spyda180190, Dan Tierney, Dan Harrison, dan, / laughingonmydeathbed, dananananicole., Daniel Carling, daniel Dickerson, Darren Hare, Dave / daveistheholidayarmadillo, David Coppin, Dean / Deano W, Dee. / xxpanhead_ princessxx, deejay / dani, Dil / dilfarooq, Dina Galino, Dirty Harry / harrynizim, Dirtybob and the missing persons list, Dizraeli, djdaddums / Mark Martin, DJ Liam, DJYeo! / Yeohan Kim, dod morrison / dmphotographyaberdeen, Donna mcbryde, doods, Doria / doriaspace, double cee, Dougle / claresaysdancewithme, Dub FX, Dub Pistols, Ducklingski-Photography, Eddie Griffiths, el; / Eleanor Fell, Eleanor Wilson, ELFiCAKES™, Elizabeth Jane / Elizabeth O'Donoghue, Elliott / Elliott Gledhill, Emily, Emily Hunt, Emmykins..=D / emma patmore, Ewan Paton / Ewan Paton Photography, Extraordinary Hatrack, Fanny Enqvist, Faye Taylor, *The Feline Pirate Drummer.!* / Toni Heron, Felixxx[x] / felix moore, Fergie :) / fergii_x, FilthyGorgeousNo1, Flappy™, Fletch / jessiebabe_x, Flick Eykyn, FOREVER CHEW, Francesca Knight, Frank B, Freckles / Claire Turner, Freckles / emily w, Fredd!!! / freaky_fredd, Fresh Sushi, Freya Elliott, Gary / sid_the_legend, Gayface / Jennifer Hawes, GEM / madam_mashed, Gemma Robinson, Gentleman's Dub Club, George Ratcliffe, georgia :) / georgiepoo101, G!mM!ck / gimmick_91, Ginger Bread Men, Glenn / djtriggah, Glitches, Goodenough, Graham Johnston, GRIZZERLY Ben, Gui Carotti!, Hal / Hal McCutcheon, haiiiii shan / shanybaby_ox, Hannah / hmc_33, [Hannah]-[why so serious?] / hannah james, Hannah Lanfear, hannibal / doodleheart, Harvey Cogs Photography, Hatty Richardson, Heather (is happy), Helen Inglis, HILDAMAY, Holly / xxx_hollii_xxx, Horsefire, Ian Severn, IDEALBEATS / Gav Beaton, IguanaWithAPie / Kate Evans, imi- The great imisaurus rex!! / Imogen Downham, I'mSoHuman / Jasmine Wallace, In-Fluence, Ivan Nuñez, izzy burnett, Jacknife / Jamie Martin, Jake Outrageous / Jake Gallagher, James Yacomen, Jamez Perry, jamie Gordon, Jamie Keir, Jane Boyd, Jasmine / magick_firefly, Jason Dalgliesh, Jay Kimber Lawson-Pearce, jen Spence, Jennifer Jones, Jenny B. Goode™, Jenny Ellwood, Jeremy Ismael, jess evans, Jessica Joanne Photos, Jessie Simmons, Jim Gellatly, jimm / j_imm_y, Jimmy / jimmylove25, jim'n'arlene / Jimarlene Roond-ye, Jinxie / noiamweasel, JLNStudios / Jennifer Nilssen, Jo Problems, Joanna Dunn, Joanne Walker, Joanie Eaton, Joe™ / Georgina Tyson, Joe Brailsford, Joe Driscoll, Joel.K… / Jason Mraz, john be, Johnny Blue / Johna, Jon / dolores_delargo, John Sweeney, Jon Kennedy, Jonny Baker, Jordan Mckenzie, JoWan / jowanhayes, Jox McRox, Junkyard Scientists, JustLikeHeaven / tabikat89, Kadaitcha.Envisions.Catastrophe / Kate Carlin, Kara Jackson, karen Mair robinson, kathryn / Kat D, katie / eitakxxkatie, katie greswell, Katie Leonard-Smith, KayJ Stamford, Kayleigh Jones, KEA - hyphen - RA / Kea-ra Jackson, keeeeeeri / kennycooper_07, Kelly Mackie, Kelly-Anne Smith, Kesah / Kes simmonds, Kevin Baxman, King Awesome! / Rob Thompson, king tom! / Tom King, Kirsty Davin, Kitch / President God, kitty / kittypenny, Kristie / kristiecantsing, Kristy!! / kristy dugdale, Kudaushe Matimba, laid back in the sun, LAIRYLOVE / CHrIs Sharpe, lameyloves.kenai+uts+nmm+bsf+themundens+immercia / lameyxx, Laura Priestley, Lauren Taylor / Nwcl.auren, Laurie;; / Laurie Perkins, Lé Cunningham / martin_cunni, LeahLovelyStuff / leah b, Lee Robbo, Lees / Leesa Watkins, Lesbian Bedsit, Liam Minett, Liam Strachan, Libbi Greenham, Lily Ward-Collins, lilyandhearts; / lily mclaren, Lindsay / lindsaylovesindie, Lindsay(Linzi) / weareglitterchic, Lisa Duncan, Liviarrr! / randomnosity, Liz, Lizzie Ferdinando, lj. / loveshackbabyyyyyy, lolly Conway, Lolwyn / Olwyn Dignam, Loopy Geek No.1 =] / Lucy Beards, Lorna, lottee dawson-meade, Lucas Diamond, LucieLinonophobia / Lucie Austin, Lydia marsh, Luke Taylor, lydia… / xxlydiax, Lynz! / barroomheroine, Majajaj, Majortones, Mandy, Marieee / marie_louise_xo, Mark Hellcock, mar.leme / tinkyishere, MaRiLeNa Über Alles, CrazyDrZenith / Mark Hall, Martin Noble, marty blount, mary / watkaaa, Matt Bentley, MC Xande, Megany,

Melissa / melissaaaaargh, MerryJerry™ [Paid], METRIC, Michael Claassen, michael ~FFL~ / Michael Hanvey, Michelle / superherokid, Mick Yates, Midnight Circus, milly / millymuso, Miss Lacrymosa / Fiona-Lori Ferguson, Miss Matilda, Mittens / xikillyoux, MLC / Matthew Crick, Molly / mollypetts, mononoke / monica mono, Moon_cheese, Morbid Humour, Moselle Foley MPPIX Photography / Mark Sayer, MRFIZZLE™ / jazzy jef, Mr VoT, Mr. Woodnote, Mz misha / Mish Mish, nabeel, Naked Guy / will gibbs, nakit@! / Nikita B., natticakes / Natalie Harlow, Naomeh! / Naomi Ward, Ness, a New Breed of Monkey, NICK [A.T.C.] / Nick Sutton, Nicki / nickizbassface, nicola mcdonald, NIKKI DU LA LOVEDAY, Nikki Noo Narr / Nicola Walker, NoCrows, noddy / nidalj, Noemie / nonoxx, Nykolette / Nyk Wallace, Off The Block Promotions / Maria Passingham, oh, amy. / Amymarie Lucas, Oisin Lunny, Only Me, Ooh!Jess / Jessica Millar, Ottilie Phillips, Owen-Face /, Rachel Owen, [O]zzLE / Ollie Hunt, PAT OH FUK !! / that_pat, Patsie / Patricia Ruddell, Paul / desp_ised, Paul Albrecht, Phlp / Philip Ward, Phoebe / duckitsphoebe, Phoebe Leyland, pictureblue / paola bildesheim, PIG, pikku janika / janika puska, pinkbitchmel / mel pink, polly poppins / polly ward, Pooch, Praying for the Rain, Psymon / Simon Chittenden, Pulpfiction / crazylilworld, pwincess sheli / michelle whitty, Radio Enjoyment, rag doll, Rage Photography, RAMUK69 FILMS, Ratty / aowenthomas, The ®eal Mc©heese / Bill Evans, Rebecca Ferrie / bam ~+~tHe LoNeLy FaIrY~+~, Rebecca Revenge, Rebekah Johnston-Smith, Rebel Seven, Red Steve, Resident Studios, Rhymenoceros / jade flannery, Rialto Lounge, Rich / rio_king, Roberto Skarzynski, ROB!N ROCKSTÅôR™, Robyn Lyness, Roisin Murphy, Rough Gem / marleymiss, Rozzie (Miss Styk) Williams, Ryan... / iluvcreamcakes, Ryan / rybr007, Ryan Brown, Sammy Moore, San Miguel / Michael Cattermole, Sarah / sarah xox, Sarah / sarah_matex0, Sarah Buckley, Sarah Dean, sarah flower, Sarah Murphy, sarah Thomson, Sarah Winterton, Sassy {Queen Bee} / franezka, ScotsAl, Sean Dyer, SebastiAn, Shambles Miller, Shel / michmichshel, shilliam. / Abi Shilliam, Si / Simon Walker, Simon Plunket, Sidjustice / Sid Bullimore, Skye / Megan Kelly, Smerins Anti-Social Club, Sophie-Doodles / sophie Glossop, sparkles*tam / Tamsin Isaacs, Sparki Dee, Spazzy Lemon, SpecialF / Fay Woodford, Stacey Duncan, steffano corradi, Steph Graham, Steph Wright, stephen Johnson, Steve wickham, StressKitten, sub rosa / Francesca H, SUBSOURCE, SupahLee / Lee Osborne, SuperPennie, SuperSexySusie / Susie Ford, suzie mcneil, Sylvia / i_d_sylvia_b, Tamsin Roberts, tash! / Tasha Jones, Tatty 'ead [Paid] / Katie Clarke, Taylor Mitson, TED from ft.worth, thebaz / barry Delaney, Theo Jennings, Theo Thompson, This is Laura, Ti amo!!! Xxx / carinakikidi, Tig / tig999, Timo / tim_barton, Tim Lloyd, ~Tina / selbststandig, Toby Jepson, Tom Wall, Tom Bandfield, Tom [dcg], Tom / Gashed, tony / tonydavidwood, Toon Timmermans, TRAV / Megan Travers, TrixyDee, Tuna Lamps, TY-RRELL / Kerrie Tyrrell, Uglypunk, unaslim, The Undercover Hippy, (undisclosed), Very Very Venkman, Vic Frankowski, Vicious Vixen / Abigail Merrick, Vicky Ní Húbhain, Vixxx designs / Vickie Kay Morgan, VJ Donkie / Donnie Tam, Walkway, Wendy / listening-2-u, Wookie! / Craig Xavier McConville, THE XCERTS, Yan Rajalot, yasmine, Yellowxander™ / Nik Alexander, Zoe Edwards, zoey sadler

@aanightingale, @Abougu, @alsoknownasbuds, @bobgotlieb, @bonnieb01, @burnmysaucepan, @campscamp, @charliesachs, @_ClaireWill, @claudineb, @cooper_town, @danieldevine, @doulooklikemary, @dearsuperstar, @E_to_the_A, @eddyTM, @Eelus, @EmmaColez, @TheFagCasanova, @gdpreston, @giftofnature, @gpants, @hairycornflakes, @iamcoxhead, @jamieONEILL_xz, @JBenni, @Jess1210, @jimgellatly, @j0hncore, @jonnyred, @Julianne166, @Karenorbit, @KalimochoFests, @lizziebaby, @lopuk, @markbmb, @MarshaVa, @martino_edwardo, @mattpat1989, @Maz4624, @mbenney, @MrWheal, @nathandainty, @neil_mccormick, @nuttyphoto, @paille69, @paul_clarke, @Pierre_Buckleigh, @pixlink, @rashebre, @Razzu666, @RichBatsford, @RockNess, @rocketfalls1, @Roscowr, @SarahBecca18, @skinnermike, @specialf, @tcoverley, @thomasgraham, @tiraybould, @tonycuth, @tonydavidwood, @trixie, @xYASDA , @producerjacob, @Stuartastbury. @ClaireBynoe, @Dorianlynskey, @wheatles, @ Xx_J3SSi, @redtibs, @Faces, @jonreed, @jonoread, @ktrac, @kmkmkmkmkm, @empom, @CraigMReilly, @evenflowuk, @musicomh

Festival Annual Photographers: Dan Wilton, Steve Bliss, Monika Magiera, Sophia Schorr-Kon, Stephanie Sian Smith, Tansy Cowley, Boyarde Messenger and the IU Team. Designed by Steve Price of Plan B Studio with Nicolò Dante. Festival Annual logo designed by Brand 42.

Conceived, created and published by Independents United: Polly Aspinall, Clare Beaumont, Rachel Bishop Sunter, Ruth Clarke, Andrea Ferraz, Shevaun Haviland, Josh Jones, Frank Lampen, Bobby Mutraporn, Shilen Patel, Rob Povey, Becks Robertson, Nick Roe, Victoria Valius, Melissa Waters, Claudia Yusef. Online Editor: Bobby Mutraporn. Edited by Josh Jones and Frank Lampen.

WITH THANKS TO:

Ben Turner; Justin, Jason, Tori, Steve, Kieran and all at CC-Lab; **Jem Melluish;** **Adge and all at Brand 42;** Stephen Greene; **Lindsay Nuttall, Sophie Rouse, Barry Flanigan, Chris Harris, James Howard, Claire Higgins, Seb Underhill and all at MySpace;** Fee Gilfeather, Mrs Jones, Emily Jones, Anna Williamson and all at Oxfam; **Danny Payne, Bernie Valentine, Lucy Barber and all at Espionage;** Fraser Smeaton at Morphsuits; **Hunter Boot Ltd;** Jack Savidge and all at Friendly Fires; Ben Ramsden at Pants to Poverty and Alice Hooper at Leo Burnett; **Holly Ferguson at Never Love You More;** Jeremy Snell, Darran O'Connor, Leon Kelly and all at Butler, Tanner and Dennis; **Lu Hunt, Alan Jewell and all at Crown Music;** **Michael McClatchey and Stephen Bass at Moshi Moshi Records;** Victoria Gratton at Virgin; Fran Babb; **Megan and Richard Skipper;** Annabelle Roe; Digby Smith; **Daniel Scott and Bunmi Oke at Atlantic Books;** Helen Kogan at Kogan Page; Steve Hatch at MediaEdge:CIA; **Henry Scotland;** Mark Bramall at **Brand Inc;** Michael Jobson and Larrisa Wood at MJM; **John Hughes, Ziggy Gilsenan, Bruce Hay, Orla Bennett, Paul Kennedy and all at Get Involved;** Rob and Josie da Bank and all at Sunday Best; **Katrina Larkin and all at The Big Chill;** Hector Proud, Kate Statham, Andrew Soar, Zoe Stainsby, Megan Thomas, Sixty Gelu, Zosia Swidlicka and all at Idea Generation; **Gill Nightingale and all at Cream;** Jenni Young, **Marcus Thistleton and all at Live Nation;** Alex Darling and all at **LD Communications;** Letitia Thomas and Leila Houimli at Outpost Media; **Nick Ladd at Glade;** Vicky Beercock and Steve Arnold at Angel Music Group; Katy Emami and all at Amazing Media; **John & Caroline Giddings, Lindsay Weatherston, Julia Barratt and all at Solo;** Melvin Benn, Tania Harrison, James Kent, Tanya Pile, Neil Pengelly and all at Festival Republic; **Rory Bett, Debbie Ward and all at MAMA Group;** **Julian Butterfield, Adrian Fillary, Clare Lusher and all at Lovebox;** Jenny Fairweather and Lily Fallala at Taylor Herring; **Zoey Benjamin at Alive Advertising;** Jo Vidler and all at Secret Garden Party; Siobhan O'Dowd and Clare Byrne at POD; **Deirdre Crookes at LH Publicity;** Tom Baker, Marcus Weedon, Jack Thomas, Lucy Wood and all at Field Day;

Warren Le Sueur and Warren Holt at Jersey Live; All at Shambala; Holly de Sylva and Anna Wade at DeSylva PR; Fenella Dale, Alex Trenchard and all at Standon Calling; Geoff Ellis, Keira Sinclair and Jo Blyth at DF Concerts / TITP; Claire Ruddock and Emma Costello at Material MC; Lucy I'Anson, Fleur Jervis-Read, Davnet Doran at Cake; Paul Glossop at De-Construct; Jo Youle; Clara Suess at Burt Greener; Jim King and all at Loud Sound; Bob Angus and Dawn Woodhouse at Metropolis; Cathryn Summerhayes at William Morris Endeavor Entertainment; Cath Lovesey at Channel 4; Marcus Viner and all and Blink TV; Tim Pearson and Alex Stiles at NME; Steve Jenner at Virtual Festivals; Chris McCormick and George Smart at Festival Awards; Shoshana Kazab at Fuse Communication; Tiger Reid at Fourth Floor Music; Paddy Stewart at Dirteestank; Dizzee Rascal; Charlotte Doran and Alison Peters at Alison Peters PR; Felix Buxton; Joseph Mount and all at Metronomy; Victoria Hesketh / Little Boots; Brendon Burns; Neil McCormick; Edith Bowman; Paul Hartnoll; Tom Araya; Frank Skinner; Marina Plentl at Sony; Karen Eeles and all at the Earl Mountbatten Hospice; Chris Sweeney at The Scottish Sun; Claire Wilson; Beardyman; Tom Middleton; David Shrigley; Huw Stephens; Chris Tofu; Chris Lawson and Cat Macdonald at Absolute Radio; David Guetta; Rob Wilson and all at Lost & Found; Tristram Shackerley-Bennett, Matt the Hat and all at the Inflatable Church; Jim Gellatly; Andy Everett, Romeo and all at Radio Clyde; Zena White; Oli Isaacs at This Is Music; Simon Harper; Emma Newman; Nathan Horrocks; Stephen Adam; Ian Giles; Syan Cox; Jade Crook; Ruanne Cowley; Lorna Deeny; Elias Comnenus; Rhady Elwen; Adam Potts; Alexander Amaral-Rogers; Amanda Clarke; Anders Johansson; Angela Collins; Aviram Ben Moshe; Ceri Gough; Conor O'Sullivan; Danielle Jolly; Darren Thomas; Diana Risso-Gill; E J Seymour; Emma Lucie; Miriam Smith; Jason Parmar; Josh Jones; Karen Davenport; Kelly Irodenko; Lennart Fjell; Lindsay Marie Brown; Maddy Smith; Neil Moore; Patrick McMeekin; Paul Stewart; Peter Beck; Roxanne Royer-Evans; Simon Price; Steven Easthope; Susan McDaid; Zanne Lyttle

INTRODUCTION

96 days.

That's how long the festival season in the UK is. From pitching the first tent when the campsites opened on the second Thursday of June, to the last raggedy spaceman shuffling out of the gates of Bestival on the second Monday in September. Just short of one hundred days of partying, dancing, drinking, dressing up and desperately not wanting to go to the toilet.

This festival culture quite literally spreads the length and breadth of these islands... from the very, very top at Rockness, to the very, very bottom in the Isle of Wight, from Glastonbury in the west to Latitude in the east. Whether you're into metal or prefer sitting down to watch some poets while Grace Jones stalks about on the stage across the site, there's a festival for everyone.

And we've been at pretty much all of them to bring you this book. We've zig-zagged the country with our tents, cameras and notepads. We've sorted through thousands of photos, we've laughed through scores of stories, and we've made countless new friends. But our contribution is nothing compared to yours.

We've met every neon Morph-suited one of you, every hotdog, every single swarm of bees, lions, tigers, tree frogs, lizards, all 30,000 men wearing dresses and legions of festival fashionistas. Each

of you has brought something unique to the summer and added together you've created this book.

Put simply: you're a big bunch of posers, but we love you.

We made Festival Annual '09 for you. We wanted to document the total nonsense and fun that we all experience in various fields around the UK each summer. Rain cannot dampen our spirits, and we laugh in the face of mud. When we have to tighten our belts there are many things in life we'd sacrifice before giving up on a weekend at a festival.

We hope that we've managed to capture some of that festival atmosphere to get us all through the dark days of winter. Soon we'll be preparing for the next 96 days in the sun, getting ready to have a cider in our hand, our excitement building as the days lengthen, and we wonder which fields to visit in 2010.

Wherever you end up, look around and you'll find someone with a camera standing right next to you. Give them a smile, and know that you're making next year's Festival Annual.

festivalannual.com
myspace.com/festivalannual
twitter.com/festivalannual

ISLE OF WIGHT
DOWNLOAD
ROCKNESS
GLASTONBURY
T IN THE PARK
LATITUDE
LOVEBOX
SECRET GARDEN
GLOBAL GATHERING
CAMP BESTIVAL
FIELD DAY
STANDON CALLING
THE BIG CHILL
V CHELMSFORD
V WESTON
SHAMBALA
CREAMFIELDS
READING
LEEDS
ELECTRIC PICNIC
BESTIVAL

@specialf
Wristband on and I am off!!

@mbenney

I've packed too much, I've packed not enough, it's a rollercoaster of emotions #IOW

There's a lot of men in kilts
this year...

Going to a festival with your mates is better than going on holiday. It's cheaper, you get to see all the bands that you love, you don't have to hang out with your friends all the time as you can go off and do different things and it's a safe environment. When I went to the Isle of Wight Festival for the first time, when I was younger, it changed my life. Suddenly I found all these other people who enjoyed the same music as I did that I'd listen to in my bedroom on vinyl LPs. I didn't know they existed. You go to a festival and you can talk to a stranger because it's a shared experience. You go to a football match and you're scared shitless that the guy's gonna smack you in the face. There's no other experience which is such a shared experience as a festival is.

- John Giddings, Isle of Wight Festival Promoter

@specialf

The red arrows just flew past! Again!

The Earl Mountbatten Hospice is the only hospice on the Isle of Wight and is situated opposite the IOW festival site. We were asked in 2004 by the promoters if we would like to come along and raise money there. The first year we went with collecting boxes and gave away small sunflowers – which is the emblem of the hospice movement – raising £600. The following year we thought about trying to sell something a bit more festival oriented, hence the large sunflowers. We now have them personalised with "IOW Festival" and the year. This proved a great idea as they have now become quite a collector's item and people instantly know we are raising money for the hospice. It has now been four years of selling sunflowers at the Isle of Wight Festival as well as at Bestival, and we have raised an amazing £72,000 towards the care of our patients.

- Karen Eeles, Senior Fundraiser, Earl Mountbatten Hospice

someone just tried to pinch a giant
hay bale from the hive at "iowfest"

day and night and day merging together, need breakfast for punctuation #iowfest

DOWNLOAD

Download is THE festival for metal – especially for European metal. Every time that we've played it's been a really good experience. Playing in front of a shit load of people is amazing. It's an awesome sight and it's an awesome feeling knowing that they're all watching you, listening to you play.

I remember there was one year when we nearly didn't make it because our flight got cancelled. We hired a private jet and we ended up playing in the blue tent instead of the main stage. That was kind of different for us. It was jam packed and fucking crazy.

We really enjoy festivals because we can just go out there and play and not be too uptight about the performance because everyone's partying.

The crowd is fucking amazing at Download. Every time that we've done it, the shows have been huge with the mosh pit going on. The crowds are so into the fact that they're there to party, they're always amazing.

- Tom Araya, Slayer

I'm so tired, I'm up to go for an impromptu day trip to Download festival today. It's warm already and it 7am, I cant imagine the temp later

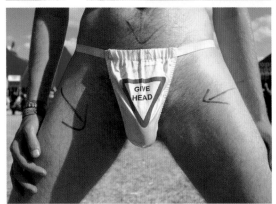

TIMMY - "i fell asleep getting a hand job from a girl at download festival"

@dearsuperstar
Just arrived at Donington for Download Festival....
This is gonna FUCKIN destroy!!!

29
Download

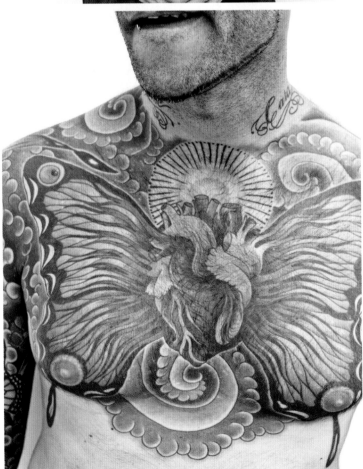

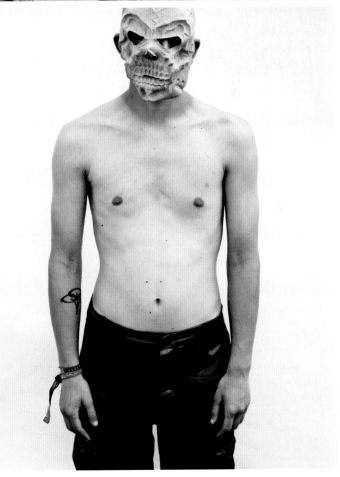

> ## "This is what happens when you burn wearing fishnets."
> - Kate Evans (posted on Myspace)

I've gone to Download every year since '04. The tickets go on sale on my birthday so I usually get it then, but this year I was moving house and never got round to it and then it sold out. In the end I bought one off my mate – I was so relieved.

This photo of me was taken on the fun house at the little fair... God I was so drunk. I've seen people try and go round it before but I've only seen one person actually do it all the years I've been. There were photographers there, and one guy tried it so I thought I would as well - I actually failed the first time. I was amazed I actually did it, people outside were cheering, I was rather proud of myself to be honest. Somehow I didn't hurt myself, but a bit further round the fun house on the slide I bashed my face and my nose was pouring with blood, they did photograph it but they never put it up – I was pulling a big grin for the photo with blood all down me!

Download was hot this year, oh my God it was hot. Bar that it was a really good weekend – the atmosphere was really good this year. Seeing Meshuggah was definitely my favourite part, as well as that night in the fun house, we were dancing on the tables in the tour bug tent, it was brilliant.

When I got back I thought I'd have a look at the MySpace site and I saw in the albums there was a Download page. I had a look and there was just a mass of colour, then I was like, "Holy fucking shit! It's me!" The people who took the photo said what it was for but I didn't remember, so when I saw it I literally jumped out of my seat, I'd told people the story but never had the pic, so I phoned everyone and told them, they thought it was well funny.

- Eddie Griffiths

Download Festival is consistently awesome, and 2009 was no exception...

Ever heard of a 'Wall of Death'? Well this happens at metal gigs when the band incite the crowd to split into two groups with a large gap between the two, and then, on the singers command, these two groups slam into each other. But the way Danish band Volbeat did it was to split the crowd in two and then they instructed the crowd to create a 'Wall of Love'. Before we knew it the crowd was running towards each other, tangling their limbs in hugs.

Really, you haven't lived until some huge man mountain of a guy dressed in a Machine Head t-shirt has run toward you, grinning, before enveloping you in an almighty, but sweaty, hug. Definitely was a weird sight, but hell, I sure left feeling good!

And this is why I love festivals, I love the sense of camaraderie, everybody joins in with everybody else – everyone is there to listen to some music, drink some beer, dance like an idiot and have some fun!

This year I wore my wellies to my graduation – it was a little nod of acknowledgement to the festival season for its role in getting me through my degree. When you're spending all day every day for the past 10 months on your dissertation, it's hard to keep motivated. Booking tickets for Download really helped me and each time I had the urge to hurl my laptop through the window in a fit of rage and frustration, I looked at the old festival wristbands on my arm and remembered good times I'd had before and also had a quick peek at the Download 2009 website to spur me on... which it did, and somehow I got a 2:1!

- Sarah Murphy, pictured above

Trivium is heaving... Bottles are flying and anticipation is palpable at the #download 2nd stage.

Greatest festival in the history of mankind...Download '09, cheers guys, wouldn't of been the same without you!xD 3

@thomasgraham
Pint in hand and it's still sunny at #rockness. View of Loch Ness from main stage is stunning.

@RockNess

this weekend - I bet
all the tourists from
all over the world
who visit Loch Ness
will wonder what on
EARTH is going on.

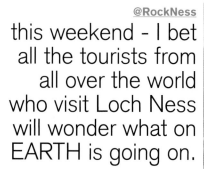

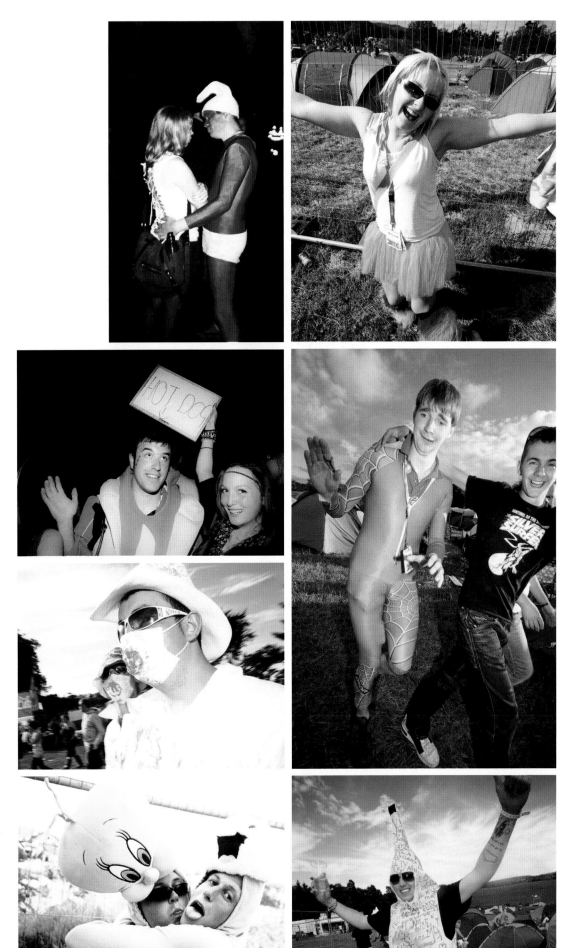

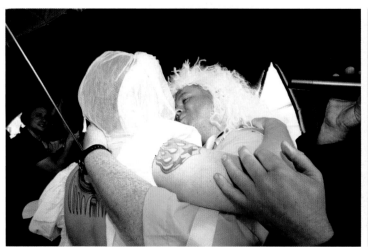 

@jimgellatly
I believe I am to get married to Vic
Galloway today at Rockness.

The Inflatable Church is an opportunity for the dishevelled to show how much they really love one another in the most peculiar way that they can, in an environment that has an ethereal, god-like quality to it. It's also an opportunity for young men to express their gender issues by putting on women's clothing and marrying each other. Which is very healthy. It's not an unholy place – it's got a real spiritual feel to it, with an underlying sense of hedonism.

- Reverend Duncan Pritchard, Inflatable Church.

one more day at ROCKNESS, I'm so sad...My landlady is gonna go mental when she sees the mud on her carpet, oops my muddy boots!!!!!

@gpants

Home from Rockness, what a blast. Back to the real world now, showers, beds, houses made of bricks not nylon

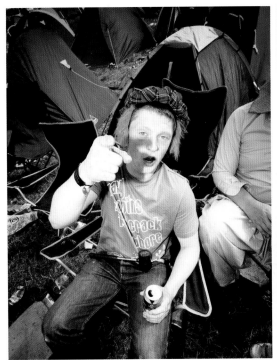

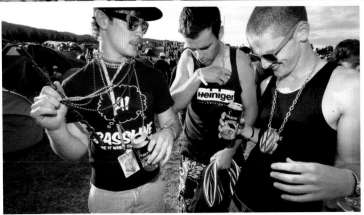

RockNess was in an other-wordly setting – being next to the loch had a fairytale quality for me. It was a great crowd of young people. It was vibrant, connected, warm as in spiritually warm, with an underlying feeling that it could kick off at any time. People were in that heightened state. It was quite tribal – it could have gone either way.

– Felix Buxton, Basement Jaxx

There's nothing nicer than having three days complete indulgence – wandering around, getting drunk, eating food, watching bands and discovering weird stuff. It's the stuff that goes on around the edges. I shouldn't be saying that being a band that plays the festivals but it's bloody true.

– **Paul Hartnoll**, Orbital

GLASTONBURY

Jesus Christ Michael Jackson is dead.

If you forgot to bring it
don't talk about it

The impression I get is that, particularly with British festivals, nobody will come away saying they had a bad time. Even people coming back from a wet Glastonbury won't come back saying it was shit, even if you find your wallet gone or your tent nicked. It's difficult for people in Britain not to enjoy them, I think if people from Spain came to a wet Glastonbury or Reading then they wouldn't enjoy it too much.

Once you're inside a festival you realise there are no sort of laws or anything, there's a real freedom. The idea is that you go there and you don't go to sleep... I guess for people who live in a city and have proper 9-5 jobs then that is a real relief, and release, for them.

– Joseph Mount, Metronomy

So, Milletts have sold out of wellies #glastonbury. Who leaves welly-purchasing until they get there? Surely they're the 1st thing you pack

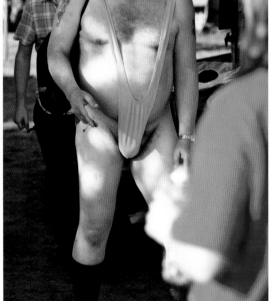

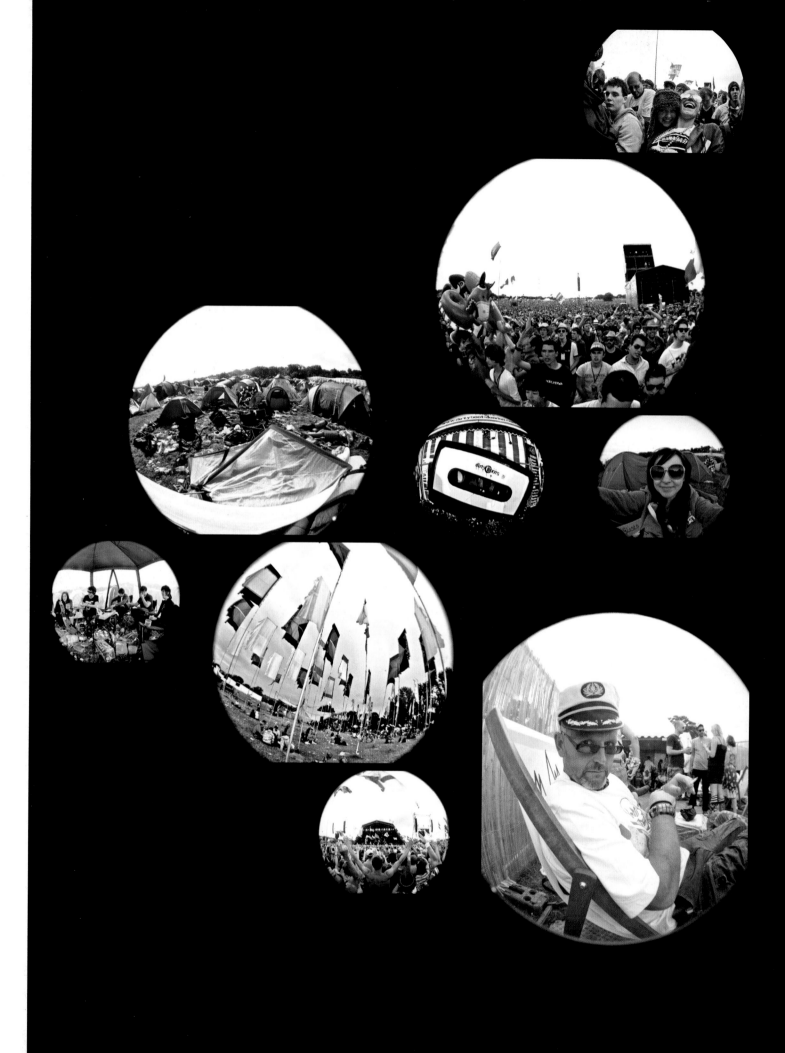

"Playing Glastonbury festival was a brilliant experience for me, there is a feeling of freedom that you don't get indoors – the crowd was great."

- Little Boots

Glastonbury '09

Peace, Love and

Rolf Harris

One year I camped in the Stone Circle with a load of mates and when we got there, we realised we'd forgotten to bring the poles for our 12-man tent. We ended up having to go round and ask people for bamboo sticks to put it up. We were there from Wednesday to Monday and I remember on the last day waking up in this poxy tent an absolutely broken girl. I woke up in a puddle thinking, "This is gonna be one bad day." I went from feeling like the most amazing woman in the world ever, to feeling like absolute shit in a puddle. There are ups and downs at a festival, but that's what it's about. Last year I found this guy who was actually cooking bread in a mud oven! You couldn't hold this festival anywhere else, because it's got all the history and there's something really spiritual about the grounds it's on. You just get a sense of freedom at festivals. It's not just the music and being rock 'n' roll – it's nice to remind people not to take themselves too seriously. It's all about the pink polka dots and the silly, silly, silliness for me!

- Jaime Winstone

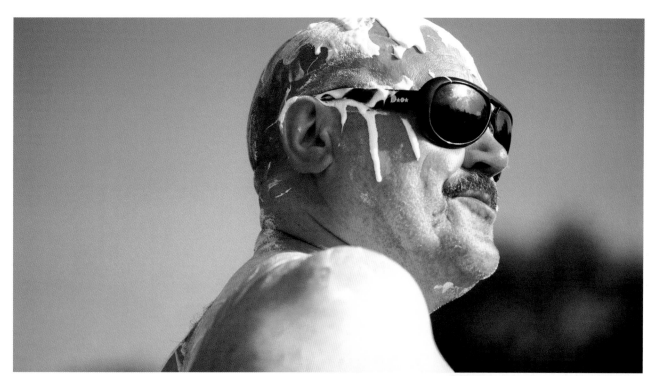

How long can a #glasto hangover last?

Anytime anyone new goes to somewhere like Glastonbury and asks me for advice on what to do, I tell them not to make any plans. In the past I've had a five-year-old girl get on stage and announce that her parents were missing. It was funny as well, as I was the only person concerned that there was a five-year-old loose. I asked her if mummy and daddy's tent was moving, and she said it was a camper van, but yes, it was moving. So obviously her mum and dad were having a shag and the kid had just gone walkabout. To this day, people still heckle me about that girl – she must be in her 20's now.... My favourite heckle at a festival was when Bill Bailey was really enjoying himself onstage and was talking about that Killers' song, "I've got soul, but I'm not a soldier". He said it was like saying, "I've got ham, but I'm not a hamster". And then everyone in the crowd started singing that to him. The entire crowd. When the whole crowd as one, as a collective conscious, tap into something and something connects with them and they all start doing it. That only happens at festivals – that sense of community.

- Brendon Burns, headlining Glastonbury '09 comedy tent

MY FESTIVAL SUMMER
OXFAM
OXFAM.ORG.UK/BLUEFACES

This summer we've painted over 30,000 people's faces at the Isle of Wight Festival, Glastonbury, Latitude, Camp Bestival, Womad, V Staffordshire and Bestival.

The Blue Faces campaign was launched with celebrities such as Jarvis Cocker, Little Boots and Fatboy Slim who had their faces painted blue and were photographed by Rankin just before Glastonbury. We did this to publicise the fact that we would be at festivals getting people to paint their own faces blue in support of our climate change campaign.

As people went blue in the face they joined our petition, which we'll be sending to the UK government. The reason we're petitioning them is because of the crucial climate change summit that will be happening in Copenhagen in December '09.

We're calling for carbon emissions to be kept level, and for fair support for the millions of people in developing countries who are already feeling the effects of climate change and for whom things will only get worse. If people want to join in this action, without painting their faces blue now, then they can still do it online.

Oxfam DIY started in our shop in Camden. The concept is that people don't need to buy new clothes. You can customise old ones or get clothes from our shops and customise them. That's what Mrs Jones (who's styled Kylie, Goldfrapp and The Killers) has been doing – getting vintage clothes and giving them her unique look.

She trained up many of our volunteers who then went out to festivals to give people amazing make-overs. Over the summer Mrs Jones and her volunteers have restyled around 1,000 people in our Oxfam DIY tents.

We also did this thing at Glastonbury called Be The Band. Mrs Jones was styling people to be the famous musicians they wanted to be – be it Lady GaGa or Bruce Springsteen.

As well as this, Oxfam has been working in partnership with Glastonbury for the last 16 years.

All of the stewards there are people we have recruited, and this year we had 80 people there painting people's faces blue. Since 1993 we have raised £2.9 million through volunteers stewarding at Glastonbury.

T IN THE FUCKING PARK. go

@Roscowr
got ... 5L of vodka, 100 fags, change of clothes, sleeping bag, chair, food... what else do I need for TITP

@hairycornflakes
Just about to set off for titp! Imodium - check, cider - check // I'm sorted :-(

@danieldevine The Mother is being a total cunt, apparently if I clean the house in the morning I might get my TITP ticket ... fuck sake! Night

@xYASDA
Bleeding hands, ripped tshirts and burnt tents already. We've only been here 3 hours

@paille69
Heading out in the sunshine for some juice!!! Tonight TITP woo hoo bevvy/bands and birds!!! Going to get blazzin :

@burnmysaucepan
NEW CLAIM TO FAME! man handled out of the front row of lily allen over the barrier! it was like a game of pass the midget! love titp

@mattpat1989
The weather at T In The Park was ridiculously good. Im sunburnt. Sunburnt in fucking Scotland. Thats like going to a Pub and drinking milk

@jamieONEILL xz
a cani believe a shagged somebody it TITP wtf srsly thts just no right

@Julianne166
TITP in less than 100 letters. Amazing, Sunny, Drunken, Hilarious, "Shag & A Shot-2 Euro" Sorry? Effy & Panda, Port-a-loos, UV Body paint...

T IN THE PARK

You ask any band what it is about playing in Scotland in general, and they'll say it's the crowd. They're not there to be impressed. They're not looking for anything – they just want to have a good time. They somehow spray that on a band who then get that energy from the crowd. It's great to watch, it's brilliant to take a step back and watch that.

It's a release for the Scottish crowd. Sometimes you go to gigs or festivals and people try to be a bit too cool for school or won't quite let themselves go, but that's not the case with any Scottish crowd, whether you're at a gig in Barrowlands or at a festival up at Loch Ness, it's just nuts. It's a total release. People have paid their hard-earned cash and they want to have a good time. It's a chance to totally unleash themselves. No holds barred. And they forget to put suntan cream on, so there's always a lot of red, drunk bodies walking around.

- Edith Bowman, Radio 1 DJ

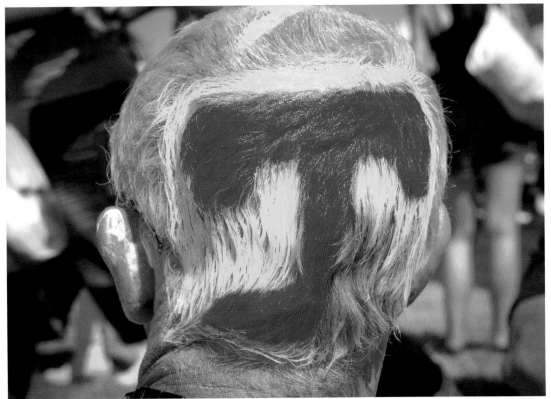

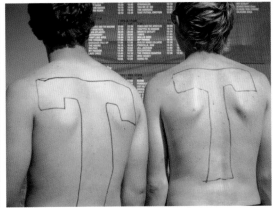

We decided to have Fancy Dress Friday a few years ago. This year I was standing by the gate dressed as Keith Richards dressed as Jack Sparrow and I reckon at least 70% of the people were all dressed up, and not just a bit of fancy dress – they were in costumes they'd obviously worked hard making.

There are people who turn up at T In The Park each year dressed as cans of Tennent's lager. It's great when a crowd embrace the sponsor. Although Tennent's are much more than just a sponsor, they've been there since the start of the event. People don't see them as a bolt on - more as an intrinsic part of the event. People paint T's on their tents and on their backs and faces. For people to do that I think is amazing.

- Geoff Ellis, founder and promoter T In The Park

I wasn't actually planning to wear any fancy dress to T In The Park to be honest...

But when I got there one of my friends told me there was a stall selling mankinis and that was the first thing I bought. After I put it on I got loads of pictures taken of me and quite a lot of people came up to me and were saying, "Oh my God!" I quite like being the centre of attention – it's good. Girls were coming up to me and taking photos. And I got a few numbers… I wore it on the Friday and the Sunday night, and on the Sunday I went for a jog around the campsite, which warmed me up a bit!

I had a fantastic time at T In The Park – Franz Ferdinand were probably my favourite. I wore it to watch them too. After I got home, my friend told me, "You're on MySpace now!" I didn't believe him, then he sent me a screenshot of it and I was like "Oh my God! That is actually me!" My friend had put it up on his MySpace and then I saw it on the homepage of Festival Annual and my friends

started contacting me. I've had quite a lot of people that I don't know adding me saying "You're that guy that's on MySpace, we really like you." A lot of people have told me that I've got a lot of courage to go around a festival wearing it. I've also had a few compliments from the ladies… It was quite a revealing piece of clothing.

I'm extremely glad I bought the mankini – I absolutely loved the attention and all the pictures, and all the looks of "What is he wearing?", and people saying, "You have to have socks down there". I had nothing down there at all, apart from what nature endowed me with! I'm definitely going to T In The Park next year, I've already got my ticket. I think I might go for a different kind of image next time though...

- Will Gibbs

I had great time at T In The Park from what I can remember! It was like my break away...

I go there every year. I love the atmosphere. Blur were amazing, and I've never seen James before and always wanted to, so seeing them was really good. I really enjoyed the Saturday night, and I spent most of the Sunday in the campsite as the crowd was so friendly. The Scottish crowd love to let loose.

I got my costume off the internet. I only really thought about getting something to wear to the festival in the couple of weeks leading up to it so I had a bit of a click about online and there it was.

I didn't get much luck with it – only from some guys. I only wore it on Fancy Dress Friday... after one day I'd had enough of the attention from all the guys! I only realised that I was on the Festival Annual MySpace site when it had been in The Sun newspaper. My mum rang me up and asked if I'd seen the paper today. I hadn't so I went and got one and that's when I found out. Everyone rang me at once. Now I'm like a local celebrity!

- Bruce McCarther

CAMPSITE SHOP
OPEN 24 HOURS
ALL CARDS TAKEN
COLD DRINKS
BATTERIES
TORCHES
FRESH MILK
BREAD
GROCERIES
PORN!
STAFF!

So good to have warm water again!! TITP was amazing!! Roll on next yr!

I'm sat alone at titp this is depressin :\

@lopuk

Last day @ #TITP
#Beetlejuice was going
2 make comeback
appearance (since every1
loved it) but can't put
makeup on cuz of the sun
burn :(

got a titp 2010 ticket. epic win

I think that a festival like Latitude has an element of peace and love about it, which not all of the modern moneymaking festivals have got. I think that there's a part of people that yearn for some sense of time where they're on the village green with a maypole.

I saw a couple snogging yesterday, very passionately, and she had a garland of flowers in her hand. I thought to myself that I could have walked into the 15th century and seen that in a village.

I think people yearn for a world where everyone's friendly – you get it at this. It's interesting what makes people happy. It's ok to get smashed and all the rest of it, but I haven't come across any hostility or unpleasantness at this festival. It's been old-fashioned peace and love.

One thing about playing a festival is people aren't paying to come and watch you play. You judge how well you've done by the amount of people who walk out. If somebody walks out at a paying gig, it's an absolute disaster, but here they're often going off to see Grace Jones or they're meeting someone to have a macro-biotic running buffet. I think I lost three from my audience and I was happy to tell myself that they had something else to go and do.

I think Latitude has probably been the best festival I've been to – it's now become my favourite - it used to be Glastonbury, then The Big Chill but now it's this one.

I walked down through the festival yesterday and all the sheep had been dyed pastel colours, and I can't remember being so pleasantly surprised. I really, really laughed. Not in derision, just in love. It surprised me and I just loved it. It made me so happy. Who'd have thought that coloured sheep could bring such joy? The sheep seemed to like it. It's not just the actual event either, the whole setting is fabulous.

I've had a blissful weekend. I don't mind the rain either. I watched Grace Jones and it pissed down and I thought, "I like this, I know I'm at a festival. It doesn't rain when you see someone at the Hammersmith Apollo or O2. But here, I know I'm out there, I'm part of the elements." So I thought the rain was a plus.

– Frank Skinner

LATITUDE

Our kids made a fortune from
redeeming the glasses at #Latitude.
Brill pocket money scheme, dad
drinks for free!

Choose What You Read was started as a reaction to the tonnes of free newspapers dished out and thrown away every day. We like to give people the opportunity to read a book instead. On the first Monday of every month we dish out second hand books, donated by the public, at selected London Underground stations. We like to give people the opportunity to choose a novel over a free paper.

We got invited to Latitude to give out free books in the wood, so we dressed up as Victorian librarians and had loads of fun. If Latitude were a pub it would be a gastro one on a hill overlooking a pretty lake. The staff would all play instruments, the landlord would be Byron and the sleeping dog would be a performance poet.

- Claire Wilson, founder Choose What You Read

#Latitude is hot. Took shelter in the theatre tent but then remembered I don't enjoy theatre. Being this uncultured is hard work.

Fascinating fact: Latitude is mud-free due to the loamy soil, which drains into the lake. Like I said: fascinating.

@nathandainty
At a rave in the woods, house music, vodka, just heard Mr Oizo - flat beat. Latitude festival is pretty cool

LOVEBOX

@lizziebaby
Saw Duran Duran do an
awesome set at Lovebox
(with Mark Ronson) and
played some wicked
volleyball today (not with
Duran Duran and Ronson).

@markbmb
lovebox day 2. foolishly
had a burito on the cusp of
swine flu outbreak. mexican
blunder.

@bonnieb01
What to wear to lovebox? Hmmm

thank you Rizla, and to everyone who came to sunday rave-in-the-park at Lovebox London. wicked sound system, rocking peeps!

@tonydavidwood
Lovebox was great -
Florence + the machine
came on as the rain
came down & umbrellas
went up

SECRET GARDEN

Secret Garden Party's secret is totally the audience. You don't go to the Secret Garden Party to see the bands – you go to be there, to wander around. I'm a veteran of too many festivals – I've been going since I was a teenager – and far too often I'm at a festival watching a band and I'm thinking to myself, "I'm just in a field, in the rain. I could be watching these in London. What am I doing here?" The Secret Garden Party has got it all going on.

It turns everybody into children. That was something that struck me – the crowd is really young, it's friendly and pretty much splattered from head to toe in face paint and decked out like they've been rampaging through a fancy dress shop. That sense of participation is really quite important at a festival. It's very liberating as people are openly celebrating each other's ridiculousness.

No one is trying to be cool – in fact the more ridiculous you are there, the cooler you are. I spotted some people dressed as raccoons dressed as pirates, a lot of 18th Century dandies and various bathing belles, a group of pharaohs and tree folk and smurfs and aliens and ghosts and a great menagerie of animals of every description.

Because there is so much to do, people are constantly moving around – looking at the sculptures in the trees and the lights on the river and also looking at the people looking at these things. People are very friendly – they talk to each other because of the barrier-breaking aspect of dressing up.

The other amazing thing is the amount of thought and imagination that's put into the surroundings. I was quite taken with a cycling pianist. When he cranked the pedals on the piano it would cycle around and he had a hula hoop girl who was dancing on top of it. He was wearing a top hat just cycling through the woods with her.

I think of it as a festival with music on the side rather than a music festival. It's really just a gathering of like-minded spirits on an adventure of their imaginations.

- Neil McCormick, music critic, Daily Telegraph

Great weekend at Secret Garden Party. Even the
swans were laid back

@Karenorbit

is thinking that was the best Secret Garden Party yet. Jarvis stage
invasion, burning Babel tower, mad hippies selling sangria, Fred
dj'ing

i am watching a 6 piece
band playing, suspended
from an oak tree.
i can only be at Secret
Garden Party.

@neil_mccormick
#secretgardenparty audience: Pirate raccoons. 18th Century Dandys. Bathing Belles. Adam & Eve. Tarzan & Jane. Pharoes. Fairies. Treefolk ...

@neil_mccormick
#secretgardenparty. Smurfs. Blue bhudda. Burlesque divas. Aliens. Ghosts. Menagerie of Human bees, wasps, snakes, bears, tigers, monkeys

@neil_mccormick
#secretgardenparty. & 1 bedraggled
rock critic with 5-yr-old space cadet on
shoulders. "Is this what your work's like
every day, dad?

Secret Garden Party was unreal. We were headlining that one. It was quite emotional as we're still quite a new band and we had about 10,000 people listening to our music. It was at night and all the lights were on. Everybody had costumes, so we fitted right in. It was the first time we'd ever done a gig like that – it was right up our street. After we finished there were all these fireworks and it was just amazing.

- VV Brown

GLOBAL GATHERING

@jonnyred
Mustn't forget to pack electro chewing gum

@gdpreston
RT Overheard by djmattcox on camp site this
morning: "I really need a wank but I can't find my
tent!" #GG09

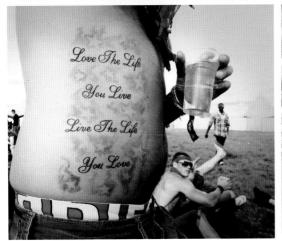

@KalimochoFests
So me, Dave, Jenny and Dave got happy in the
Polysexual Happy Hardcore tent until 6 in the
morning! Haha, 12 hour neon party people

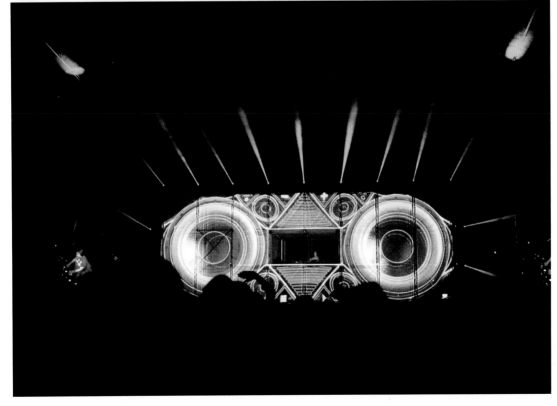

@martino_edwardo

Lost my phone, lost my wallet, lost in the music, lost for words. Global Gathering, what a weekend…

@E_to_the_A

Thoroughly enjoyed Prodigy, Tiga and erolalkan at global gathering last night ! Tune after tune it was too much !!

@cooper_town

Global Gathering was amazin at the weekend, so much shit was chatted and the tunes and decor were top notch. Can't wait for next year!

@Jess1210

first chance to say how intense and completely amazing Global was – raved my tits off till i literally ached immense!

@KalimochoFests

Have lost half a stone over weekend, clearly dancing twelve hours a day like Girls Aloud (probably) is the way forward ladies #GG09

@j0hncore

On train back from #GG09 weak, wasted and sunburnt to fuck.

@jonnyred

Heading home from #GG09 - tired, broken and disco damaged but ultimately happy. What a weekend!

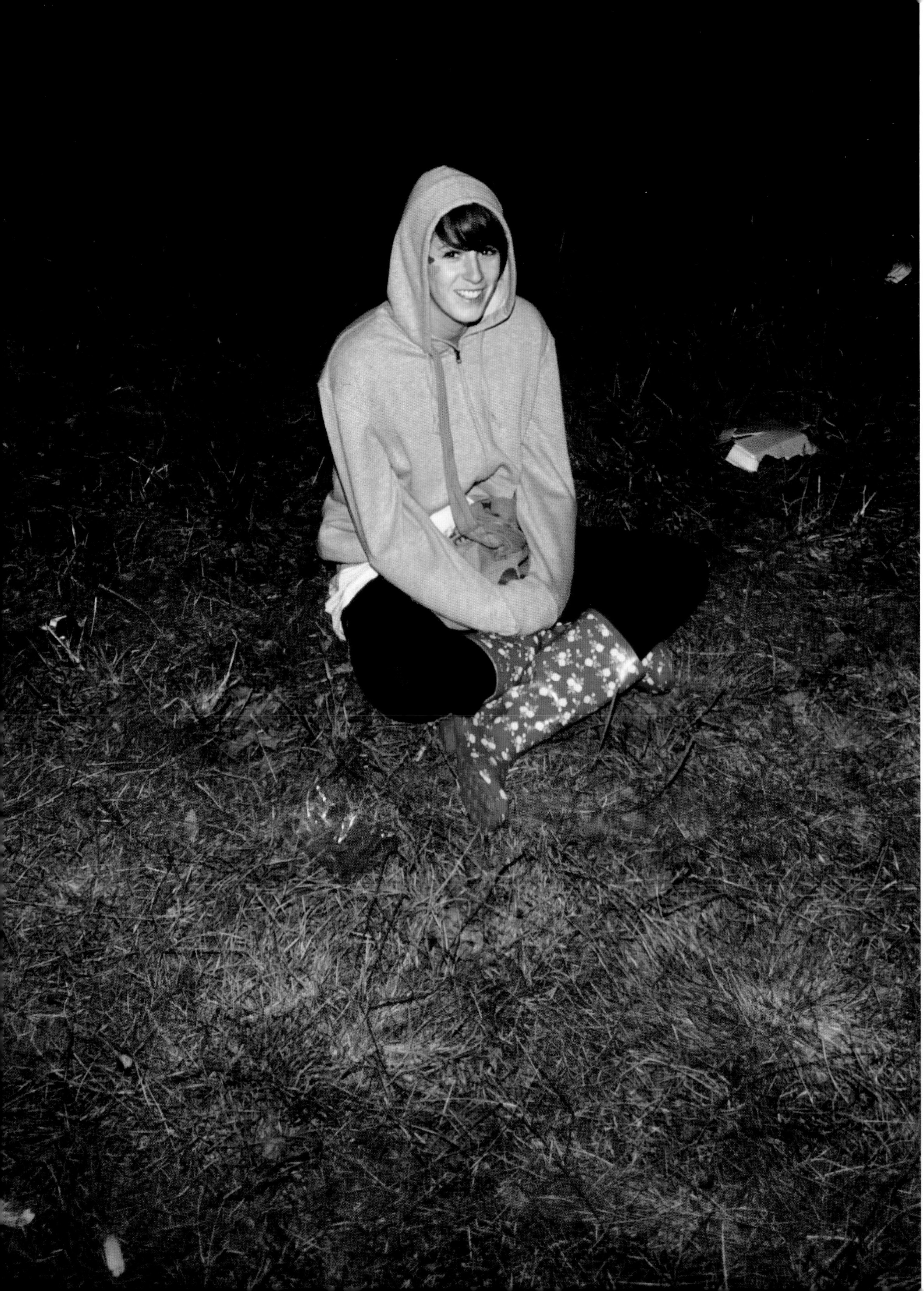

It's easy at Camp Bestival – the kids make it. If it was just adults it would be fun, but when you see all these happy, smiling faces, your hangover just goes away.

Mr Tumble's secret gig this year at Camp Bestival was one of my favourite festival moments. It was bonkers – it was a bloke putting a custard pie in his face. It's the simple things isn't it?

– Rob da Bank, Bestival and Camp Bestival founder.

At Camp Bestival there are families here that are genuinely happy. If you go to an adult show it's only adults and a children's show, it's only children.

Here they've merged it totally seamlessly. Everyone here is having a great time. That means a lot to me. I think it's so good that these things exists. I think it's the only festival like this in the world. It retains this beautiful vibe and feels home-grown with what Josie Da Bank does with the visuals. The setting has its own personality as well.

– Beardyman, Camp Bestival '09 Main stage host/Beatboxer

CAMP BESTIVAL

@campscamp

camp bestival i thank you. the perfect place to dance with your baby. i've never done colouring in during a scratch perverts set either.

@MarshaVa

Camp Bestival gig was great fun. Treading line of being rude enough for the kids and clean enough for the parents...

MY FESTIVAL SUMMER
FRASER SMEATON

FOUNDER OF MORPHSUITS.COM

I love fancy dress. I am always on the lookout for something that is a little bit different. Quite a while ago, I found an all-in-one lycra suit in a charity shop and brought it along to a boys weekend in Dublin. We had never seen a reaction to a fancy dress outfit like it, every two steps someone stopped me for a picture and everyone was asking where they could get one. We obviously weren't that bright because my two business partners and I took two years of people begging to borrow it for festivals and stag parties before we realised that it might be worth starting to make them.

Once this had dawned on us Morphsuits.com was born.

After we saw how people responded to them, we decided to bring them to the masses. It hasn't all been plain sailing, the suit I bought in a charity shop made it difficult to see where you were going. So we worked with our manufacturers to get Morphsuits just right. Now you can see where you are going, bust some big shapes on the dancefloor, or ride a bike... The other thing people like about them is that you can drink a pint through a Morphsuit... although clearly we'd never condone that!

We thought that there might not be many people who love fancy dress like us, or that we would have to explain it to people, but we don't. People just seem to love them straight away. I've been to Glastonbury, Lovebox and V this year. All three festivals were AMAZING, but just when I thought they couldn't get any better, I'd bump into a bunch of Morphs. It was like meeting my long lost brother or something. At Glastonbury we had

a 30-Morph congregation at dawn which was quite cool and then at V we made a morph human pyramid, which was classic.

We had no idea how popular they would be. The first batch was only 200. It was when they sold within a couple of weeks that we realised that they might be pretty popular. We have sold a few thousand now, including sending them to France, Norway, Holland, USA, Canada, Australia and even China – so the Morph community is going global!

The thing that I love most is that Morphsuits has 7000 Facebook fans. The banter is brilliant and there are so many photos, which are always a giggle.

Of course we've got our eye on creating a new craze next year... We can't give away the details yet but it will be Morphsuits like you have never seen before!

FIELD DAY

I always try and book acts selectively so it's not all bands that are playing all the festivals. There was so much going on at Field Day this year, people really enjoyed the village mentality and the village fete area. I think that sums it up – people had a go on the sack racing or the splat the rat and didn't dwell on the weather because it was out of our control. People got into it. They knew that they were only there for the day and at the end of it they could go home and get into their beds.

-Tom Baker, Field Day founder

STANDON CALLING

@Eelus
Well, my chest-burster costume didn't win shit at
Standon. Some girl in lycra with a glittery camel toe
took 1st prize, typical

The Big Chill started with 500 people back around '94 or '95 in the Black Mountains in Wales. It was the real golden era for what you would call Chill Out. They brought in some healers and masseurs and organic vegetarian cuisine. It was the ingredients, I suppose, of what makes up The Big Chill today: a really diverse music selection and a friendly, personable environment. Now we've arrived at this point where we've got a fantastic location in the middle of Herefordshire, the beautiful Eastnor Castle as the backdrop and its wonderful deer park – it's a really good environment to put a festival on. I think Norman Jay – who's always been a part of it – has done a deal with the big man up there to make sure we always get good weather. Last year I did 20 years of Acid House. We had 40,000 people with their hands in the air singing along to Candi Staton and The Source. That was a wicked moment. Probably one of the festival highlights of my career – looking out over two generations of people singing along.

- Tom Middleton, DJ

THE BIG CHILL

I've been DJing in the Rizla arena at RockNess, Lovebox, The Big Chill and Bestival. It's kind of fun. All the festivals are different. I'm not really a festivalgoer. I only really go and see bands in the city. I don't like camping and I don't like chemical toilets. I'm a bit of an armchair traveller I'm afraid. Apart from the mud it's been a lot of fun. When I first did the show I didn't even know how to operate the CD players as I'd never DJ'd with CDs before. I had to ask the sound guy how to do it. I'm a bit afraid of the technology. As long as there's not any silence and it's at the right speed then it's ok.

People at The Big Chill seem a bit more artsy-fartsy, hippy-dippy, for want of better words. I think the crowd at The Big Chill suits me best being an artist and all. I guess that makes me an artsy-fartsy person. I played at lunch-time but I still had some people dancing to my set at The Big Chill, which is surely a good sign.

- David Shrigley, artist and Rizla festival DJ.

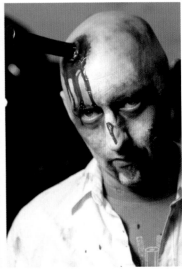

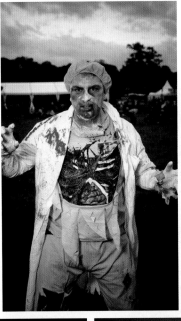

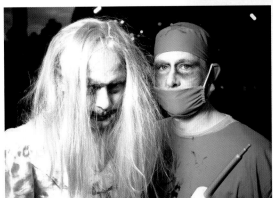

@paul_clarke
#bigchill No, I've not come as a fucking zombie. I look like this because it was pissing down earlier and I have two small kids.

V CHELMSFORD

Pants To Poverty was launched at Glastonbury in 2005 after Nelson Mandela called on a generation to rise up and make poverty history. We looked for different ways that we could communicate these issues, and principally, it's about pants. Within 36 hours of being at the festival, we'd sold 3,000 pairs of pants. Fashion is something that brings the richest and poorest together very visibly through cotton supply chains.

WIthin six months of making our first pair we'd sold over 10,000 of them without going through a single shop. Today we're working with over 7,000 cotton farmers in India, in an area known as the 'Suicide Belt', where 26 farmers every single day commit suicide. They represent what Mandela's talking about. They've been marginalised by society and pushed into poverty. We support them on lots of different levels – we help them set up projects that they own and control and we help sell their cotton into the markets, trying to get the big bastards of retail to buy ethical cotton rather than from sweat shops. We work with four amazing factories in India who make perfect, ethical cotton. We now sell our pants across 22 countries.

We look at pants as a metaphor – what's right are our good pants and what's wrong are all the bad pants that are out there. We try and get our consumers to understand the devastating impact of their bad pants and also the amazing and powerful impact their good pants can have.

The response we get from people when we're at festivals is amazing. People love the idea and the concept and get really excited about that, and people also like the design and the product. And we get to party with people in our pants all weekend...

- Ben Ramsden, founder Pants To Poverty

V WESTON

There were so many people when I played at V Festival, it was ridiculous. I was so happy being there – I'm so happy I've taken this direction in my music as I can't think of any other way I would have been able to gather a crowd as big as that and make them all jump up and down, especially when I played 'Bonkers' and 'Holiday'.

- Dizzee Rascal

@JBenni
is hanging, burnt to a crisp and has no voice...
and i LOVE IT!! Roll on next year! #vfest

MY FESTIVAL SUMMER
STEVE JENNER
FOUNDER AND DIRECTOR OF VIRTUALFESTIVAL.COM AND THE UK FESTIVAL AWARDS.

I've been immersed in festivals – hundreds of them – all year round, for the past decade that I've been running Virtual Festivals (and more recently the UK Festival Awards). Today they remain as fascinating, wondrous, thrilling and magical to me as ever. Like a mythical odyssey, I always leave a festival knowing a bit more about both myself and the outside world. Take this year, for example...

My festival season began at the Brighton Festival back in May, where I saw people crowd surfing at an acoustic performance by The Levellers. There was an intensity given off by the band and the crowd that I hadn't experienced for a long time. Something was definitely in the air.

I got my next dose of it at RockNess, on the hauntingly beautiful shores of Loch Ness in Scotland, in June. 35,000 young people having an ecstatic time on ground where thousands were slain a quarter of a millennium ago. It was the best atmosphere I've ever encountered

at a festival – pure, unrefined good times, with the music very much the backdrop. This wasn't temporary escapism, but a coming together of youth en masse to create a sense of positivity, inspiration and hope that stays with you when you get back to the real world. That's what a true festival does. Even the rain granted the site a compassionate reprieve for the most part.

That's more than can be said for Glastonbury two weekends later, which received its customary fix (or two) of biblical torrents. Yet the ground remained miraculously dry, as if to reassure us that storms (whether meteorological or economic) are transient and need not cause lasting damage to our spirit. The largest contemporary music festival in the world seemed to glide on a revitalised wind. My 11th Glastonbury was the friendliest, most relaxed, strangely efficient and uplifting one yet. Perhaps that's what took Damon Albarn over the edge when he collapsed in floods of tears on-stage during Blur's magnificent reunion on the Sunday night.

Next was Guilfest. Like an eccentric seaside town, this Home Counties jewel has let the boutique festival revolution of the last few years pass it by and remains virtually unchanged since I first visited in Virtual Festival's birth-year of 1999, lending a quaint charm.

The weather wasn't so approving, however, and the rain showed no mercy throughout a brutal 24-hour assault in the middle. This created one of the most extraordinary and British festival spectacles I have ever beheld – a couple of hundred souls dancing and slipping around with Dunkirk determination in the sheeting rain in front of a dry and oblivious Brian Wilson who was singing along cheerfully to 'California Girls', occasionally calling out "Hello London!" I was mesmerised by the moment and got soaked to the bone just watching.

Eccentricity was taken to another dimension altogether a couple of weeks later at Secret Garden Party, which is essentially a four day advanced training course in how to properly lose yourself. This year they'd built an impressive 'Tower of Babel' on an island in the middle of the lake. This was the venue for Virtual Festivals' tenth birthday party, which we had to row and punt people out to in boats and gondolas. It was very special. A couple of nights later, they blew the tower up. Then there was a huge paint fight. Bonkers.

A week after this saw something else very special – the birth of a brand new festival. It was called Sonisphere and it took place at Knebworth Park – a venue that had been waiting to house a festival for a long time. As a powerful cast of rock cognoscenti rolled across its main stages, crowned by the mighty Metallica, the infectious mist of joy, confidence and hope that had been building up at all the other festivals I'd visited throughout the summer permeated every corner of the stunning site.

My festival summer has left me with a new spring in my step – revitalised, refocused and ready for whatever the world will throw at me. It's a genuine, life-affirming natural high and I remain hopelessly addicted, counting down the days until next summer. As Michael Stipe once sang, "I'll take the rain."

Shambala packing progress update: practical items: 5, sequin dresses: 6, pearl necklaces: 2, bottles of champagne: 5. That is all.

SHAMBALA

@RichBatsford
Cream tea and strawberries on top deck of london bus, listening to the beach boys and looking out over the shambala festival. Xx

CREAMFIELDS

Decision made:
Creamfields, tonight. This
is the craziest 96 hours
of my life.

At Creamfields we were up against the pumping trance muscle of Tiësto – so the crowd wasn't massive, but they were hugely enthusiastic. Someone was even compelled to throw a pink furry boot at the stage.

At dance festivals I get anxious about the gaps between songs – people aren't ready for silences. Also they don't get the silly band thing of going off then coming back on for an encore, so when we first left the stage everyone strolled off to Tiësto. Fair enough I guess, it'll teach us not to use hackneyed rock and roll conventions as part of our set.

- Jack Savidge, Friendly Fires

@ClaireBynoe
Had such a good weekend! Creamfields was immense!
David Guetta is so amazing, he is my sexy biittccchhh haha

This is a music festival. It's never going to be anything else. I remember standing on the stage with Huw Stevens and he said that Reading should have the strap line: "No fucking circus acts here."

It's about the bands and it's about the fans. We're just the bit in the middle connecting the two. It's the energy of the crowd that defines Reading. It's unexpected for the bands. You can see it in their faces when they come on stage. There is no indifference at Reading. If they like you, they will appreciate you. If they don't, they will certainly let you know.

– Melvin Benn, Reading & Leeds Festival founder and promoter.

It's great seeing people here on the Thursday night looking at the running list for the weekend and trying to work out which bands they're going to see. You can't kid people who come to Reading. They know their music. They're really into it. This year Florence & The Machine and Pendulum were my favourites. It's great to see the performers from the smaller stages come through. There's a certain badge of honour here to either go down well or be bottled off. I've booked over 1500 bands here at Reading, but I'll always be remembered for Daphne & Celeste. I only put them on as a bit of a laugh, and it's all people talk about to me.

– Neil Pengelly, Reading & Leeds Festival booker.

READING

There's a flag in the crowd. WHAT WENT WRONG? #reading09

@producerjacob
a total of 8 hours sleep, bruises, too much cider,
spooning, swimming pool runs, od's on pro plus and
RADIOHEAD! #reading09. fkn amazing.

When I first went to Reading I'd never seen anything like
it. You've got three days to cram everything in and the
memories you're left with stick with you forever. I've still got
a drumstick from that Reading year, rotting away upstairs.
Because we all love music so much, getting to go camping for
the weekend, hang out with mates AND see some of the best
new bands around is an absolute joy. Beats going on a package
holiday to Mallorca too.

– Huw Stephens, Radio 1 DJ

Home time, havent slept, but didnt
catch fire, so swings and roundabouts
really #reading09

@MrWheal
YORKSHIRE! YORKSHIRE! YORKSHIRE!
YORKSHIRE! YORKSHIRE! YORKSHIRE!
YORKSHIRE! just getting ready for leeds fest and
weekend of that

LEEDS

@EmmaColez
@leedsfest this time tomorrow and if i'm not drunk I will see it as the biggest fail of my life, next to not seeing the Spice Girls ofc.

Toilet report: First one of the day, it looks like a excrement themed Jackson Pollock exhibition in here. Grim. #Leeds09

Toilet report: 2nd go, there is a shit tinted footprint on the wall and it looks like a psycopath's aquarium in the bowl.

Toilet report: 3rd trip. I *REALLY* don't want to talk about it. Bad. Se7en bad. #Leeds09

@TheFagCasanova
Toilet report: (hopefully)
Final pee. Went alfresco.
Quite pleasant. Why
did this not occur to me
sooner? #Leeds09

@TheFagCasanova
The toilets aren't so bad.
I find the more drunk you
get, the less they bother
you, have you never been
to one?(festival, not toilet)

@Pierre Buckleigh
LeedsFest lesson No.1: wellys + really hairy fucken legs = pain and bald patches. Why was i not warned?!?!

MY FESTIVAL SUMMER
LOST & FOUND
NONSENSE FACILITATORS

Lost & Found is FUN... and FUN isn't a word – it stands for a Feeling of Uninhibited Nonsense. It's something that allows people to be completely free and release themselves from overactive self-awareness or the social conditioning that restrains them. It allows them to act like children and let themselves go. We do this through various ways – normally by looking like absolute wallies. That really helps, because if we're making fools of ourselves then no one can be worried about looking like an idiot.

It's all about the people who come and interact with us. It's not about us acting, showing off and looking crazy. It's about welcoming people into an environment of nonsense. We don't have any political agenda or any particular religious point of view. It's all done for the aim of fun, good vibes and positivity.

When you think of organised fun you get those horrible feelings of being made to do things that you really don't want to. We never do that to people, it's a very free space where people can come along and get involved if they want to. A lot of people rediscover things that they'd forgotten about – like a game of rounders after a big night out, or musical statues. It's all about being a child – it's all about having pure fun. British people really know how to have a good time and I think when people from other countries come over they're quite surprised that we all get down. And they find it hard to keep up.

It all started when my best friend Oscar and I met Kate Jackman from Bestival while we were at The Big Chill and she invited us to go along and do something there. With this great opportunity, we came up with the idea of a Lost & Found swap shop, which was a mobile place for people who'd lost stuff – but to get it back, they had to swap it with something else. Other ideas came after that, like massive scrabble tiles on the end of big poles, which then evolved into a hat scrabble game, which then evolved into more games. Lost & Found is this living organism that keeps regenerating ideas. It's a real collective where everyone has input into the things we do. Every time we do something we learn more about what it is for people to have fun and to play, and we get better and better at having a good time. Obviously we really enjoy ourselves in what we're doing and everyone parties.

Our ideas come from all over the place – binocular football comes from seeing it on the TV show Takeshi's Castle – but generally they start with puns. For example, the moustache courier service, where the tagline was "We'd love to stick around but we mous-tache…". We all had moustaches on and went around delivering parcels. We thought that we needed to make it as fun as we could for ourselves and also the other people, so it worked on two levels. There was us going round on crazy bikes delivering parcels, but we also had delivery dockets with specific delivery criteria on them like 'the woman that's just fallen over', or 'the man in the queue who looks like he hasn't been to bed'. We had to find these specific scenarios and then we'd give them the parcel. These people couldn't believe they were being given something so specific when they'd just fallen over or whatever. That was gold.

I love all of the games we do, but I think my favourite, from the having-a-dream-and-seeing-it-happen point of view, has to be giant scrabble. We took it to the guys at Bestival and they didn't think it was going to work, but we were stubborn as we thought it was a great idea. We worked really hard on building all these massive props. Just to see that moment – when these words were being put together and people were all playing together and everyone could see it – amazing. It always starts off with rude words, but they can get quite sophisticated. At one point four guys formed a line to say P-I-N-T and then went to the bar. They'd never met before but all had a drink together. We also get quite long sentences like W-I-L-L S-W-A-P S-E-X F-O-R D-R-U-G-S.

I'd say that Bestival is my favourite festival. They tick all the boxes really, it's really well organised, the fancy dress is incredible, the atmosphere is amazing. The guys really care about what they're doing and they put loads of love into it. They're really right on with what they do and they're a wonderful crew.

We were at RockNess and Shambala, we were the Bestival Bluecoats at Camp Bestival earlier in the year, and then at Bestival we ran the Cosmonaut Training Academy. We put the crowd of space cadets through their paces – training with us to become cosmonauts, getting their space faces on, learning how to beat the laws of physics with aunty gravity, proving they can survive on space fodder at the dehydration station, testing their mental resolve in inner space and crawling through the wormhole into outerspace, taking a leap of faith in musical mooning and of course surviving the pressure that was the rinse cycle.

And it was…. a small 'Yep' for flan and one giant bleep for Flan-kind…

Our overall dream is to form a Lost & Found old people's home where we're all going to be when we're older and it's going to be the funnest place ever.

– Bobby Lost, Director of Nonsense and co-founder Lost & Found

I think the quality of mud at our festivals is better than mud elsewhere around the world. I think you'll find the mud in other places doesn't quite stick to you so much or it turns very easily to dust – it's the weather, it's the weather isn't it? That's the thing we have at our festivals and it can be so changeable. I was at the Electric Picnic in Stradbally in Ireland and one day it was nice and sunny, the next day it was chucking it down, and that's what they're all about, dealing with the weather, and being aware of the weather, and do as I always do and make sure you're playing in a big tent...

- Billy Bragg

ELECTRIC PICNIC

BESTIVAL

Watching ballet at a festival. With a girl on crutches. Kinda sums
up the weirdness that is #bestival

Bestival is as much about the effort the crowd puts in as all the effort we make as organisers. The spirit of fancy dress encapsulates this – people go to town on their costumes and don't take themselves too seriously, which adds to the vibe of the event. As promoters we create a playful and exciting environment and make sure there's as much colour and off the wall entertainment as is possible, and the Bestival crowd returns the favour by supporting us year after year. It's a win-win situation for everyone.

- John Hughes, co-promoter Bestival and Camp Bestival

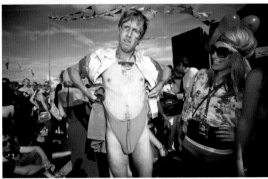

At Bestival we had a stall right by the main stage and sold about 800 pairs of pants. On the Sunday, we set the Guinness World Record for 'the most people gathered in one place in their pants', with our Pant Flash of 295 people, which more than doubled the previous record. Next year at Bestival we're planning on simultaneously breaking every single pant-based record there is.

Right at the end of the festival, just before they blew up the tower, there was a guy in a gold spandex bodysuit who was wearing every single pair of mens pants that we do. The last thing he did before it blew up was take off each pair of pants and then jump off the platform just before they set fire to it.

We had an amazing party at our stall selling our pants right the way through the festival and it all culminated with the Pant Flash on the Sunday and then the pants on fire thing... It was amazing.

– Ben Ramsden, founder Pants To Poverty

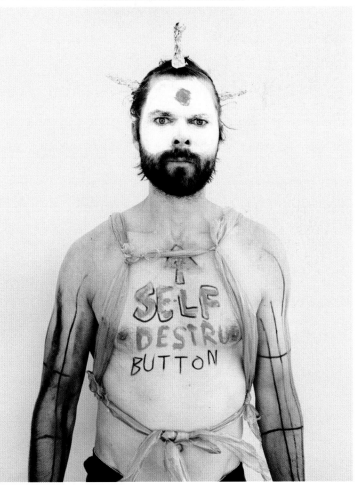

Festival goers are incalculably better dressed than in the early 90s. #bestival

The first time we went to Bestival, we decided to camp there with everyone. The trouble was we had no idea that they have the whole fancy dress day thing on the Saturday. In an insane stroke of luck I was borrowing a van off a friend of mine and in that van there was a dressing up box in it. Oscar from the band put on a badger mask, a leather jacket and a string of plastic sausages around his neck. He also had a packet of Dairylea Dunkers.

We ended up losing him and got back to the tent about 4am. We found him about a foot away from the tent. He still had the badger mask on, but had lost the sausages. The last thing he could remember was climbing up on the roof of the café and eating his Dairylea up there all on his own...

I guess the thing with all festival stories is that you really had to be there.

– Joseph Mount, Metronomy

PHOTO CREDITS:

ISLE OF WIGHT

p10-11: Frank Lampen for Festival Annual

p12: Simon Plunket

p13 top four: Chris Cowley (www.contrast.tv); bottom two: Frank Lampen

p14 top and second row: Chris Cowley; all others Frank Lampen

p.15 skeleton: Chris Cowley; all others Frank Lampen

p16-17 boy in blue glasses: Chris Cowley; all other Frank Lampen

p18-19 Isle of Wight girl: courtesy of Solo; all others: Chris Cowley

p20 top left: Monika Magiera for Festival Annual (monikamagiera.blogspot.com); all others Chris Cowley

p21 top: Monika Magiera; bottom: Frank Lampen

p22: Frank Lampen

p23 bottom left: Chris Cowley, all others: Frank Lampen

p24: Frank Lampen

p25 first row right and second row left: Chris Cowley; second row right: Matthew Purser; bottom row: Simon Plunket; all others by Frank Lampen

DOWNLOAD

Photographed for Festival Annual by Dan Wilton (danwilton.co.uk)

Additional photos:

p29 bottom middle: Tom Medwell (tommedwell.com);

p32 top: Kate Evans

p33 top left Ryan Martin; top right: Sarah Murphy; second row left: Michael Claassen; second row right Kate Evans; third row: Michael Hanvey; fourth row left: Stefano Corradi; fourth row right: Daniel Dickenson; bottom row left: Sarah Murphy; bottom row right: Megan Kelly

ROCKNESS

Photographed for Festival Annual by Steve Bliss (stevebliss.blogspot.com | in-colour.co.uk)

Additional photos:

p38-39: Paul Campbell

p40 top left: Jamie Keir

p48 bottom right: Sarah Dean

GLASTONBURY

Photographed for Festival Annual by Dan Wilton and Steve Bliss

p58-59: Dan Wilton (danwilton.co.uk)

p60: Steve Bliss (stevebliss.blogspot.com | in-colour.co.uk)

p61 top: Roxanne Royer (myspace.com/ducklingskiphotography); bottom left: DW; bottom right: SB

p62: SB

p63: SB, except top right: DW

p64-65 people in seats and lady with blue hair: SB; all others: DW

p66 top: SB; all others: DW

p67 top left and second row left DW; all others: SB

p68 top row left: DW; right: SB; second row left and right: SB; middle: DW; third row left: DW; centre and right: SB; bottom row: SB

p69 second row middle and bottom row left: SB; all others: DW

p70: DW

p71 middle row left: Sam Moore; bottom row middle: Katie Clarke; all others DW

p72 top row centre: DW; left and right: SB; middle row: DW except for middle row right: Adam Thompson; bottom row: SB

p73: Michael Eavises: Dod Morrison (myspace.com/dmphotographyaberdeen); Red Heart: SB; all others: DW

p74-75: Kate Greswell

p76: Little Boots: Felicity Ieraci; Union Jack: Mick Yates; setlist: Christine Joseph

p77: middle row left and bottom row left: SB; all others DW

p78-79: Jessie Simmons (jessiesimmons.com)

p80-83: DW

p84: top: Roxanne Royer; bottom left: SB; bottom right: DW

p85: top row and middle row centre: DW; all others SB

p86: Mark Martin / djdaddums (myspace.com/djdaddums)

p87: top row: SB; bottom row: DW

p88: top left and bottom left DW; top right and bottom right: SB

p89: top: DW; all others: SB

p90: SB

p91: top: DW; bottom: SB

p92: all DW

p93: top: Dod Morrison; bottom right: DW; all others: SB

p94: middle left: DW; middle right: Kerrie Tyrell; all others: SB

p95: DW

p96: Roxanne Royer

p97: Jessie Simmons

MFS: OXFAM

All photographs by Sophia Schor-Kon (sskphotography.co.uk | sskclick.blogspot.com) for Festival Annual

T IN THE PARK

Photographed for Festival Annual by Dan Wilton (danwilton.co.uk)

Additional photos:

p102 bottom left: Clare Beaumont for Festival Annual; bottom right: Jordan McKenzie; middle row: Alison Malcolm

p103: middle right: Liam Strachan; bottom: Jordan McKenzie

p104 top and middle row: Clare Beaumont

p105 top left: Dod Morrison (myspace.com/dmphotographyaberdeen)

p106: Clare Beaumont

p108 top row left, top row right, middle row right: Clare Beaumont; middle row middle: Zoe Edwards

p110 bottom row right: Katastrophy Girl; middle: Clare Beaumont; right: Jordan McKenzie

p111 top row left and fourth row right: Alison Malcolm; top row middle and right, second and third row right, fourth row left, fifth row middle, bottom row middle: Clare Beaumont

p112 bottom row left: Dan Wilton; bottom row second right: Alison Malcolm; all others Clare Beaumont

p113 bottom row left: Dan Wilton; top row second left: Alison Malcolm; all others Clare Beaumont

p115: bottom row middle: Clare Beaumont; bottom row right: Alison Malcolm

p116 top left: Clare Beaumont

p117 top left, top right, bottom left, bottom right: Clare Beaumont

LATITUDE

Photographed for Festival Annual by Dan Wilton (danwilton.co.uk)

Additional photos:

p120 bottom right: Dan Harrison

p125 middle second from left: Susie Ford; bottom right: Hannah Lanfear

p127 top left: Becky Cooke

p135 Hannah Lanfear

LOVEBOX

Photographed for Festival Annual by Frank Lampen

Additional photos:

p136 bottom: Tamsin Isaacs

p137: Tamsin Isaacs

p139 bottom left: Tamsin Isaacs

p140 top right: Tamsin Isaacs

p142 bottom left and middle: Tamsin Isaacs

p143 all Tamsin Isaacs except bottom right: Tamsin Roberts

p144 middle row left: Tamsin Roberts

p146 middle left and bottom right: Tamsin Isaacs

SECRET GARDEN PARTY

Photographed for Festival Annual by Dan Wilton (danwilton.co.uk)

Additional photos:

p151 bottom right: Monika Magiera for Festival Annual (monikamagiera.blogspot.com)

p153: Monika Magiera

p154 top and middle rows: Frank Lampen for Festival Annual

p155 bottom row left and right: Frank Lampen; bottom row middle: Monika Magiera

p156 top right and bottom right: Monika Magiera

p157 middle right: Monika Magiera; bottom left: Frank Lampen

p158 bottom right: Frank Lampen

p159 bottom right: Frank Lampen

p161 bottom left and right: Frank Lampen

p163 top right: Monika Magiera

p164 top right, bottom left and middle: Monika Magiera; middle right and bottom right: Frank Lampen

p165 bottom left and middle: Monika Magiera; middle row right: Frank Lampen

GLOBAL GATHERING

Photographed for Festival Annual by Steve Bliss (stevebliss.blogspot.com | in-colour.co.uk)

Additional photos:

p177 bottom middle: Clare Beaumont for Festival Annual

p178 top left and middle, and bottom left: Clare Beaumont

p179 all except bottom right: Clare Beaumont

CAMP BESTIVAL

Photographed for Festival Annual by Sophia Schor-Kon (sskphotography.co.uk | sskclick.blogspot.com)
p196 top left and bottom right: Vic Frankowski (frankowski.com.au) for Get Involved

MFS: FRASER SMEATON

p202: Frank Lampen for Festival Annual
p203 left: Dan Wilton for Festival Annual; right: Sophia Schorr-Kon for Festival Annual

FIELD DAY

p204 middle right: Monika Magiera for Festival Annual (monikamagiera.blogspot.com); bottom left: Bronia Stewart for Field Day; bottom right: Tom Medwell (tommedwell.com); all others: Clare Beaumont for Festival Annual
p205: middle right: Bronia Steward; bottom: Vic Frankowski (frankowski.com.au) for Get Involved; all others Monika Magiera

STANDON CALLING

Photographed for Festival Annual by Nick Roe

THE BIG CHILL

Photographed for Festival Annual by Dan Wilton (danwilton.co.uk)
Additional photography:
p208 top: Nick Roe for Festival Annual
p210 fourth row right and bottom right: Nick Roe
p211 bottom left and right: Nick Roe
p213 top right: Ben Gilbert
p216-217: Tim Lloyd (timlloydphoto.com)
p218 all: Jonny Baker (flickr.com/photos/jonnybaker)
p219 top: Jenny Ellwood (flickr.com/photos/coolkiddo)

V CHELMSFORD

Photographed for Festival Annual by Boyarde Messenger (boyarde.com)
Additional photography:

p223 second row, second from right and bottom right: Ruth Clarke for Festival Annual
p224 top left and bottom middle: Ruth Clarke
p227 bottom left and right: Ruth Clarke
p229 bottom right: Aidan McManus; bottom row, second from left: Ruth Clarke
p230 second from top on right hand side: Ruth Clarke; bottom middle: Aidan McManus

V WESTON

Photographed for Festival Annual by Frank Lampen
Additional photography:
p234 bottom right: Clare Beaumont for Festival Annual
p235 top left: Clare Beaumont
p236 bottom middle and right: Clare Beaumont
p238 bottom left: Bobby Mutraporn for Festival Annual; bottom right: Clare Beaumont
p239 top right: Bobby Mutraporn
p240 bottom left: Bobby Mutraporn
p241: too right: Bobby Mutraporn, bottom right and bottom middle: Clare Beaumont

MFS: STEVE JENNER

Peter Corkhill for VirtualFestivals.com except for p245 bottom: James Yacomen

SHAMBALA

Photographed for Festival Annual by Stephanie Sian Smith (stephaniesiansmith.co.uk)

CREAMFIELDS

Photographed for Festival Annual by Frank Lampen

READING

Photographed for Festival Annual by Dan Wilton (danwilton.co.uk)
Additional photography:
p261 top: Marc Sethi (marcsethiphotography.com)
p262 top right and middle row, middle column: Marc Sethi

p263 bottom right: Marc Sethi; top row middle: Vicki Morgan
p266 all except bottom left: Marc Sethi
p268 top and middle row right: Marc Sethi
p269 bottom left: Marc Sethi
p270 bottom left and right: Marc Sethi
p271 bottom three images: Marc Sethi

LEEDS

Photographed for Festival Annual by Monika Magiera (monikamagiera.blogspot.com)
Additional photography:
p272 middle column left: Chris Leck
p280 bottom right: Clare Beaumont for Festival Annual

MFS: LOST & FOUND

Sophia Schorr-Kon (sskphotography.co.uk | sskclick.blogspot.com) for Festival Annual except for
p284: Hannah Lanfear
p285 bottom centre: Frank Lampen for Festival Annual

ELECTRIC PICNIC

Photographed for Festival Annual by Tansy Cowley (tansycowleyphotography.com)
Additional photography:
p288 top left: Aaron Corr (flickr.com/photos/strangelove1981); middle row left: Moselle Foley (mosellefoley.com)
p289 top left: Sarah Buckley (flickr.com/photos/sarahbucko)

BESTIVAL

Photographed for Festival Annual by Dan Wilton (danwilton.co.uk), Sophia Schorr-Kon (sskphotography.co.uk | sskclick.blogspot.com) and Frank Lampen
p290 top left: Tamsin Isaacs; top right: DW; left middle: FL; bottom: Vic Frankowski (frankowski.com.au) for Get Involved
p291 top and bottom left: SSK; bottom right: FL
p292 top centre: SSK; all other top: DW; middle left and centre: FL; middle

right: Fay Woodford; bottom centre: Tamsin Isaacs; bottom left and right: FL
p293 top left: SSK; centre and right: DW; second row left: FL; second row centre: SSK; third row left: FL; fourth row left: SSK; fourth row right: Tamsin Isaacs; bottom left: SSK; bottom centre and right: FL
p294 top left: FL; top centre and right: DW; second row centre: DW; second row right: SSK; third row from left to right: FL, FL, SSK, DW; bottom row from left to right: FL, DW, DW
p295 top right: FL; all others: SSK
p296 fourth row right: courtesy of Pants to Poverty; all others SSK
p297 top left: DW; all others SSK
p298-9: DW
p300 top left: FL; top right: DW; all others SSK
p301 top left: FL; top right and bottom: SSK
p302 top: DW; bottom: SSK
p303 top left and bottom: FL; middle right: DW; all others SSK
p304 top right: Tamsin Isaacs; bottom left: Marie Berry; all others: FL
p305 top left: FL; all others: DW
p306: DW
p307: top left and right and bottom right: DW; second row rightand third row right: SSK; all others: FL
p308 top: Fay Woodford; bottom: FL
p309 bottom right DW; all others FL

COVER

Cover and back cover photographs by Dan Wilton for Festival Annual (danwilton.co.uk) except for Morphs: Frank Lampen for Festival Annual
Inside flap from top: Vic Frankowski (frankowski.com.au) for Get Involved; Frank Lampen; Marc Sethi (marcsethiphotography.com); Frank Lampen

UK FESTIVAL AWARDS 2009

19th Nov 09

Indigo2, O2 Dome, London

http://www.festivalawards.com

The UK Festival Awards are the annual 'Oscars' of the contemporary music festival industry and remain the only such event dedicated to recognising and celebrating the colossal human effort that goes into producing the UK's world-leading music festival scene.

Originally founded in 2004 by the team behind Virtual Festivals.com, the Awards have since exploded from an online-only endeavour into a full-scale gala event, featuring live performances from international artists, with more than 1000 of the most influential people in the industry coming together for one night only, to let their hair down and celebrate. In keeping with Virtual Festivals' ethos, the UK Festival Awards allow the fans to set the standard with both the shortlists and final winners being decided by public vote. Last year, more than 350,000 public votes were cast.

This year's awards ceremony takes place at the Vue Cinema in the O2 complex, and Festival Annual is proud to be the partner for the Fan Photo Award.

For more information, to vote and get tickets: www.festivalawards.com